| DATE DUE | | | |
|---|---|---|---|
|  |  |  |  |
|  |  |  |  |
|  |  |  |  |
|  |  |  |  |
|  |  |  |  |
|  |  |  |  |
|  |  |  |  |
|  |  |  |  |
|  |  |  |  |
|  |  |  |  |
|  |  |  |  |
|  |  |  |  |
|  |  |  |  |
|  |  |  |  |

# The Toronto Blue Jays

## Baseball Champions

Bob Italia

Published by Abdo & Daughters, 4940 Viking Dr., Suite 622, Edina, Mn. 55435.

Library bound edition distributed by Rockbottom Books, Pentagon Tower, P.O. Box 36036, Minneapolis, Minnesota 55435.

Printed in the United States.

Cover Photos:  Allsport
Inside Photos:  Allsport 13, 17, 18, 20, 23, 24, 27, 28, 29, 31, 32, 33, 35, 36, 38.
                SportsChrome 4, 6, 9, 11, 15, 18, 38.

**Edited by Rosemary Wallner**

**Library of Congress Cataloging-in-Publication Data**

Italia, Robert, 1955-
    The Toronto Blue Jays: world champions of baseball / written by Bob Italia.
    p.  cm. — (The Year in sports)
Summary: Presents highlights of this Canadian team's 1992 season which ended with a world championship.
    ISBN 1-56239-239-5
1. Toronto Blue Jays (Baseball team--History--Juvenile literature. 2. World series (Baseball)--History--Juvenile literature. [1. Toronto Blue Jays (Baseball team)--History. 2. Baseball--History.] I Title. II. Series.
GV875.T67I83 1993
796.357'64'09713541—dc20                                        93-13084
                                                                    CIP
                                                                    AC

# Contents

Great Expectations. . .Again........................................5

That Championship Season (Weeks 1-14) ..................7

The Division Title (Weeks 15-26)..........................19

Chasing the Pennant ................................25

The World Series ................................29

Final Major League Standings—1992 .....................37

Glossary ................................................39

*With Jack Morris on the team,*
*Toronto had high hopes for the 1992 season.*

# Great Expectations. . .Again

In 1992, baseball experts picked the Toronto Blue Jays to finish first in the Eastern Division of the American League. This idea was nothing new. Toronto had a talented team. And experts usually picked the Blue Jays to win their division. But could the team win the World Series—something that a Canadian team had never done?

In 1991, Toronto won their division, but lost to the Minnesota Twins in the playoffs. Critics called the Blue Jays "chokers," meaning they couldn't win the important games. In 1992, Toronto was eager to prove the critics wrong.

Before the 1992 season, Toronto signed former Minnesota Twin Jack Morris. Morris, a right-handed pitcher, was the 1991 World Series Most Valuable Player (MVP). Right-handed pitcher Dave Stieb had recovered from off-season back surgery and the coaches expected him to return to the pitching rotation.

With lefties Jimmy Key and David Wells, and righties Morris, Stieb, Juan Guzman, and Todd Stottlemyre, the starting rotation looked strong. In 1991, Blue Jay pitching led the American League in Earned Run Average (ERA) with a 3.50 mark, shutouts (16), and a club-record 60 saves. And with relief pitchers like Tom Henke and Duane Ward waiting in the bullpen, many people considered the Jays' pitching staff one of baseball's best.

Toronto's outfield was also one of the league's strongest. All-Star Joe Carter played left or right field, and the fleet-footed Devon White played center field. The outfield also included rookie Derek Bell, Minor League Baseball's Player of the Year. In 1991, Carter led the team in Runs Batted In (108) and home runs (33).

The infield looked just as strong. There was All-Star second baseman Roberto Alomar, first baseman John Olerud, third baseman Kelly Gruber, and shortstop Manuel (Manny) Lee.

Alomar and White finished 1-2 on the team in batting. They combined for 86 stolen bases and won Gold Glove Awards for fielding excellence. Alomar led the team in hits (188), stolen bases (53), and batting average (.295). White led in runs scored (110).

Greg Myers and Pat Borders were expected to share the catching duties. If the starting lineup faltered, Toronto had a strong bench to rely on. Newcomers Candy Maldonado and Dave Winfield battled for the Designated Hitter (DH) spot. Both could play outfield. Veteran infielder Rance Mulliniks also waited for his chance to play.

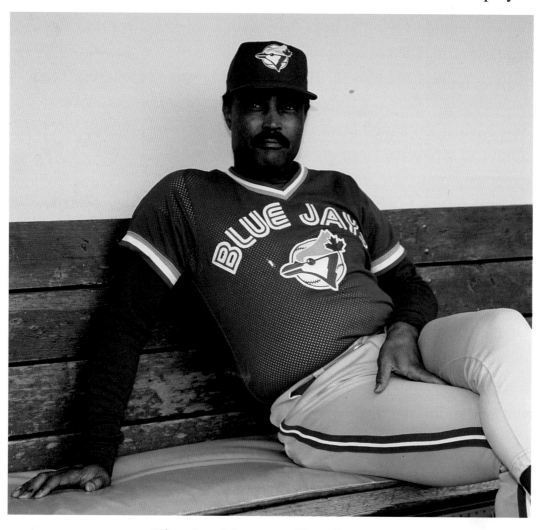

*Blue Jay Manager Cito Gaston.*

# That Championship Season
# (Weeks 1-14)

The Blue Jays started the season with a bang as they went 5-0, their best start ever. Jack Morris won two games. In the Opening Day game in Detroit, Michigan, against the Tigers, Morris threw 145 pitches in nine innings for the complete-game victory. Then he went seven innings against the Baltimore Orioles in Toronto. The Jays won easily, 7-2.

Morris wasn't the only star that first week. Catcher Pat Borders hit three home runs in his first four games. His most dramatic was a ninth-inning, game-tying, 418-foot shot in the Jays' home opener against Baltimore. John Olerud reached base on 11 of 15 plate appearances, including six hits and five walks. Kelly Gruber was 6 for 20 in the first five games with two doubles, a triple, and a home run.

| Standings | | | | |
|---|---|---|---|---|
| Through games of April 12 | | | | |
| EASTERN DIVISION | | | | |
| **Club** | **W** | **L** | **Pct.** | **GB** |
| **Toronto** | **6** | **0** | **1.000** | **—** |
| New York | 5 | 0 | 1.000 | .5 |
| Boston | 2 | 3 | .400 | 3.5 |
| Baltimore | 2 | 4 | .333 | 4 |
| Cleveland | 2 | 4 | .333 | 4 |
| Milwaukee | 2 | 4 | .333 | 4 |
| Detroit | 0 | 6 | .000 | 6 |

Pitcher Juan Guzman equaled his career high with 10 strikeouts against the Tigers in a 3-1 victory. And Jimmy Key went seven innings and threw 117 pitches in the home opener. He gave up three runs in the first inning, but then shut down the Orioles the rest of the way. Reliever Duane Ward earned saves in his first two appearances against the Tigers.

Dave Winfield began asserting himself as the Jays rolled along in April. Winfield went 3 for 3, including a home run, against the New York Yankees in Toronto. Winfield helped the Jays to a 6-1 home stand and a 10-3 record. After 20 games, Winfield was hitting .351 with two homers and 10 RBIs. The Blue Jays record ballooned to 15-5, good enough for first place in their division. It was the most victories the team ever had in April.

Though Winfield turned 40 on May 26, he clearly wasn't acting his age. He doesn't see himself as an older player, either.

"Each year," Winfield said, "you see if you can hit line drives, hit home runs, run the bases. You say, 'Hey, I can still play with these guys.'"

"He plays hard all the time," said Toronto Manager Cito Gaston. "That hasn't changed. He runs everything out, just like he was a rookie."

| Standings | | | | |
|---|---|---|---|---|
| Through games of April 26 | | | | |
| EASTERN DIVISION | | | | |
| Club | W | L | Pct. | GB |
| Toronto | 15 | 5 | .750 | — |
| New York | 12 | 6 | .667 | 2 |
| Baltimore | 11 | 7 | .611 | 3 |
| Milwaukee | 8 | 8 | .500 | 5 |
| Boston | 7 | 9 | .438 | 6 |
| Cleveland | 7 | 13 | .350 | 8 |
| Detroit | 6 | 13 | .316 | 8.5 |

Winfield was in his nineteenth season. He is first among active players in career home runs and RBIs.

Though Winfield was off to a great start, Roberto Alomar was grabbing all the local sports headlines. After 20 games, Alomar led the league in hitting (.397), runs (19), hits (31), and RBIs (19). During that stretch, Alomar had four three-hit games and two two-hit games. In the final week of April, he reached base nine times in a row, including seven consecutive hits and two walks.

Other hitting stars included Joe Carter, who had a 16-game hitting streak. And surprising to the team, Pat Borders scored 14 runs in his first 20 games.

Not to be outdone, the bullpen turned in great numbers. The relief pitchers had a 5-1 record with seven saves and an ERA of 2.65. Duane Ward led the way with four saves.

*Dave Winfield got off to a hot start in April.*

Dave Stieb finally returned to the starting rotation. Though he lost 7-2 to Cleveland in his first game, the Jays were happy to have him back. It was Stieb's first start since May 22, 1991.

Juan Guzman showed that Jack Morris wasn't the only dominant pitcher on the team. Guzman finished April with a 3-0 record. Dating back to last season, Guzman had won 13 of his last 14 decisions.

Toronto experienced difficulty when May arrived. In Week 4, they went 2-4 as their overall record slipped to 17-9. In a nine-game span, the pitching staff gave up 14 homers. Morris was the biggest victim. In his first six starts, he had given up eight home runs.

Still, Toronto had plenty to be happy about. Roberto Alomar continued his torrid hitting. He went 23-for-44 in an 11-game hitting streak. And Winfield had hit in 11 games in a row.

The most encouraging sign came from Dave Stieb. Stieb won his first game in almost a year. He held the Milwaukee Brewers to three hits in a complete-game, 3-1 victory on May 3. His last win had been May 11, 1991, against the Chicago White Sox.

The Blue Jays turned around dramatically in Week 5. Winfield capped an 8-7 comeback victory over the Seattle Mariners by hitting his tenth career grand slam with two out in the ninth. That week, Winfield's 17-game hitting streak stopped. He was 24-for-62, including 4 doubles, 4 homers, and 10 RBIs. It was the longest streak in the league to date, and Winfield's personal best.

The Jays finished the week with a 5-2 mark and a 22-11 overall record. Juan Guzman picked up two more wins, improving his record to 5-0 with a dazzling 1.61 ERA. In his last 29 starts, Guzman had posted a 15-1 record.

After Guzman pitched a 4-1 victory over the California Angels on May 10, Angels Manager Buck Rogers said, "We ran into a buzz saw. I'm surprised we got one run off him. He's one of the good young

*Juan Guzman showed that Jack Morris*
*wasn't the only dominant pitcher on the team.*

pitchers in the game today. He has a good arm, and now he has it all."

After going 3-3 in Week 6, the Jays had even more difficulty in Week 7. On May 23, in a game against the White Sox in Chicago, the Blue Jays committed five errors, one short of the team record. They finished the week with a 2-4 record, 27-18 overall.

But the Jays had a few bright moments. After going three games without a home run, the Jays hit four in a 8-7 victory over the Minnesota Twins on May 20. The next game, in Chicago, the Jays hit four more against White Sox ace Jack McDowell.

| Standings | | | | |
|-----------|---|---|---|---|
| Through games of May 24 | | | | |
| EASTERN DIVISION | | | | |
| Club | W | L | Pct. | GB |
| Baltimore | 26 | 16 | .619 | — |
| **Toronto** | **27** | **18** | **.600** | **.5** |
| New York | 23 | 19 | .548 | 3 |
| Boston | 20 | 19 | .513 | 4.5 |
| Milwaukee | 20 | 21 | .488 | 5.5 |
| Detroit | 19 | 24 | .442 | 7.5 |
| Cleveland | 14 | 30 | .318 | 13 |

In the same game, Juan Guzman continued his great pitching. He improved his record to 6-0, giving up only five hits and striking out seven in eight innings. Since June 15, 1991, Guzman had made 30 starts with just one defeat.

"Everything he throws up there is live," said Chicago Manager Gene Lamont of Guzman. "He's just a real good pitcher."

Roberto Alomar returned to the spotlight in Week 8. In a game against the White Sox in Toronto, Alomar hit a solo home run to break up a scoreless game as the Jays won 3-0. The next day against the White Sox, Alomar drove in the Jays' first run to tie the score in the eighth inning. The Jays eventually won 2-1. At that point in the season, Alomar was hitting .452 with runners in scoring position. He helped the Jays that week to a 4-1 record, 31-19 overall.

Stumbling through Week 9 with a 3-3 mark and a 34-22 overall record, the Blue Jays had recorded more victories than any other team

*Roberto Alomar was a bright spot in May.*

in the American League. But the Jays were not happy with their performance so far.

"We've been fortunate to win as many games as we have," said General Manager Pat Gillick. "We haven't hit consistently. Other than Guzman, our pitchers haven't put a good stretch together since early in the season."

They were also getting outplayed. In a 3-game series against the Orioles in Baltimore, the Oriole outfielders robbed the Blue Jays of three homers. Two of the homer-saving catches were made in the Orioles' 1-0 victory on June 5.

"Everybody knows what they've got — good pitching and defense," Jimmy Key said of the Orioles. "If they get that pitching all season, they'll stay with us."

The pitching did come around in Week 10. Jack Morris defeated Boston Red Sox ace Roger Clemens 4-0 on June 11. It was the first Toronto victory over Clemens since June 4, 1988. Guzman followed Morris' performance with a 6-2 victory on June 14 as the Jays finished the week with a 5-2 record, 39-24 overall.

Joe Carter was the hitting star that week. He went 14-for-29 with four homers and eight RBIs. But Kelly Gruber, once a fan favorite, began hearing boos at Toronto's Skydome. In a 10-game stretch, Gruber had only five hits in 39 at bats for a .128 average.

The Jays were also concerned about Dave Stieb. Stieb was 3-6 and had recorded only one victory in his last five starts. In his last 32 innings, Stieb had allowed 19 earned runs.

"We're looking for a pitcher," said Pat Gillick. "We're talking to a couple of clubs, but there's nothing close."

To help the situation, the Jays considered moving relief pitcher David Wells to the starting rotation.

The pitching staff did not improve the following week. Dave Stieb and Todd Stottlemyre were becoming weak links in Toronto's

14

*Joe Carter was the hitting star in Week 10.*

starting rotation.  Since May 4, Stieb had a 2-5 record.  Stottlemyre was 1-5.  The Jays' other starters were 14-7.

Guzman continued to be the brightest pitching star.  In a game in Kansas City on June 20, he limited the Royals to one run on five hits in eight innings.  He improved his record to 9-1.

Gruber's slump continued.  He hit just .188 for the month with only one base hit.  "I'm trying to play through (the slump)," he said.  "But I'm not doing too well.  All I can do is give 100 percent and hope the ball falls in."

Despite the slump, Gaston remained committed to using Gruber.  He was a solid third baseman with playoff experience.  Gaston knew he would need Gruber in the lineup if the Jays made it to the World Series.

"I know his average is down," said Gaston of Gruber.  "But look at his RBIs (26).  Kelly has had a lot of big hits for us.  I think we need Gruber to win this thing, even if it's just for his defense."

Toronto marched toward the All-Star break with a vengeance.  In Week 13 the Jays posted a 5-1 mark, scoring 51 runs.  Toronto's 49-31 overall record was the best in club history through 80 games.

In a game against the California Angels in Toronto on July 3, the Jays set a club record by collecting nine consecutive hits to open the third inning.  They fell one short of the American League record.

### Standings

Through games of July 5

EASTERN DIVISION

| Club | W | L | Pct. | GB |
|---|---|---|---|---|
| **Toronto** | **49** | **31** | **.613** | **—** |
| Baltimore | 46 | 34 | .575 | 3 |
| Milwaukee | 42 | 37 | .532 | 6.5 |
| New York | 40 | 40 | .500 | 9 |
| Boston | 37 | 41 | .474 | 11 |
| Detroit | 37 | 45 | .451 | 13 |
| Cleveland | 33 | 48 | .407 | 16.5 |

The Jays eventually won 10-1. In the same game, Dave Stieb made his first relief appearance since August 16, 1988.  He pitched two scoreless innings.

On July 4, the Jays spotted the Angles a 6-1 lead. Then they rallied for an 8-6 victory. Tom Henke recorded his 200th career save.

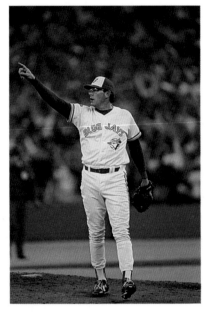

*Tom Henke recorded his 200th career victory on July 4.*

Only 12 other pitchers have reached that milestone.

"I'm glad to get it out of the way," said Henke. At the time, he had 14 saves in 15 chances.

Alomar fell behind Kirby Puckett of the Minnesota Twins in the batting race. But Alomar drove in 15 runs in a 14-game stretch. Juan Guzman and Jack Morris were a combined 20-4. But the remaining starters were 16-19. Kelly Gruber was sidelined with a strained knee. He wasn't scheduled to return until after the All-Star break.

In Week 14, Jimmy Key pitched his first shutout of the season as he limited the Seattle Mariners to six hits. David Wells moved into the starting rotation and went 2-2 with a 4.15 ERA. Wells liked his new role as a starter and wanted to stay there. Manager Cito Gaston kept the option open.

"It depends on Wells," he said. "If he pitches well, he stays there."

The Jays scored 68 runs in winning nine of the first 10 games in their longest home stand of 1992. But in the final series before the All-Star break, the Jays scored only two runs in three games against the Oakland A's. Still, they were in first place and looking eagerly toward the second half of the season.

Roberto Alomar was named to the All-Star team. So was Joe Carter and Juan Guzman. At the break, Alomar was hitting .323 with 45 RBIs. Carter had 19 home runs and 63 RBIs. Guzman (11-2) led the league in ERA (2.11) and strikeouts (122).

He also held opposing batters to a .185 average, the best mark among American League pitchers. His 11 victories tied a club record Dave Stieb set in 1990.

One Blue Jay who did not make it to the All-Star team was Dave Winfield. He was disappointed. "I earned a spot and deserved to be there," he said. At the break, Winfield was hitting .303 with 14 home runs and 47 RBIs.

The Jays were grateful that Winfield and Morris were on their team. Morris had posted a 10-3 record.

"I think we probably have a little better lineup than the nine we put on the field last year," said Gaston. "One thing's for sure. We've definitely improved the D.H. department this season. Dave Winfield's been tremendous for us."

| Standings | | | | |
|-----------|---|---|---|---|
| Through games of July 12 | | | | |
| EASTERN DIVISION | | | | |
| Club | W | L | Pct. | GB |
| **Toronto** | **53** | **34** | **.609** | — |
| Baltimore | 49 | 38 | .563 | 4 |
| Milwaukee | 45 | 41 | .523 | 7.5 |
| Boston | 42 | 43 | .494 | 10 |
| New York | 42 | 45 | .483 | 11 |
| Detroit | 41 | 48 | .461 | 13 |
| Cleveland | 36 | 52 | .409 | 17.5 |

*Roberto Alomar, Joe Carter, and Juan Guzman*
*made the 1992 All-Star team.*

# The Division Title (Weeks 15-26)

The Blue Jays started the second half slowly. In 11 games, they went 5-6 for an overall record of 58-40. Guzman developed tightness in his shoulder and left the game in the third inning at Oakland. He eventually went on the disabled list.

Kelly Gruber returned to the lineup and got his first RBI since June 24. Candy Maldonado became the first Jay to homer off A's relief ace Dennis Eckersley since Lloyd Moseby in the 1989 playoffs. It was Maldonado's third homer in six games. But Tom Henke could not protect the lead, and the Jays lost.

The Blue Jays woke up in Week 17. Joe Carter ended a 0-22 slump by going 5 for 13 with three doubles, two homers, and eight RBIs in a four-game stretch. Candy Maldonado had his 12-game hitting streak snapped. During that time, he was 18 for 43 (.419) with four homers and six RBIs. That week, the Jays went 5-1 to improve their overall record to 63-41.

To strengthen their bullpen, the Jays traded catcher Greg Myers and outfielder Rob Ducey to California for relief pitcher Mark Eichorn. Toronto also called up catchers Randy Knorr and Ed Sprague from their minor league club in Syracuse, New York.

Toronto took to the road in Week 18 for games in Boston and Detroit. The Jays' starting pitching was awful. They gave up 34 runs in less than 26 innings for an 11.92 ERA and went 2-5. With Dave Stieb's troubles and Juan Guzman on the disabled list, it seemed that the Jays had to trade for a quality starting pitcher if they wanted to reach the playoffs.

The Jays pitching problems continued through August. Only Jack Morris posted a winning record (4-1). In Week 20, Morris pitched against the Minnesota Twins. He held his former teammates to seven hits and one run in seven innings for his sixteenth victory.

Dave Winfield was one of a few hitting stars that month. He had four homers and 22 RBIs. Candy Maldonado's career-high 15-game hitting streak came to an end. During that time, he went 20-for-61 (.328) with four homers and 10 RBIs. John Olerud had his 10-game streak stopped after going 14 for 31 (.452) with two homers and 10 RBIs.

Toronto made a major move in Week 22. On August 26, they signed former New York Mets pitcher David Cone. Cone was one of the best pitchers in the National League. It seemed the Jays had found the solution to their pitching problems.

*David Cone joined the Blue Jays on August 26.*

Cone was hammered in his first American League game against the Brewers in Toronto. In his second game against the Twins, Cone gave up three runs in the first two innings. But after receiving advice from teammate Rance Mulliniks, Cone settled down and posted his first American League victory.

"Rance said I was pressing, I was trying to do too much," Cone recalled. "He said the guys knew I was a good pitcher and just to relax."

In the same game, the Jays got 10 hits in a row in the second inning, tying an American League record. The Jays went on to a 16-5 victory.

Before that home game, Dave Winfield was critical of the Toronto fans. He wanted them to be more vocal and supportive.

"The way it is here," said Winfield, "the teams we're attempting to beat have an advantage over us at home and are playing on neutral ground in Toronto. I know when I used to come in here with teams like California and the Yankees, I never felt any anxiety or apprehension. There was no feeling I was facing any opposition other than the Toronto club itself. You never dealt with the kind of hostile atmosphere you encountered in other cities."

The fans responded with shouts and cheers. David Cone and the Blue Jays did not let them down.

| Standings | | | | |
|---|---|---|---|---|
| Through games of August 30 | | | | |
| EASTERN DIVISION | | | | |
| Club | W | L | Pct. | GB |
| Toronto | 74 | 57 | .565 | — |
| Baltimore | 72 | 58 | .554 | 1.5 |
| Milwaukee | 69 | 61 | .531 | 4.5 |
| Detroit | 63 | 68 | .481 | 11 |
| New York | 61 | 70 | .466 | 13 |
| Boston | 60 | 70 | .462 | 13.5 |
| Cleveland | 59 | 71 | .454 | 14.5 |

The next night, Juan Guzman made his second start since returning from the disabled list. He allowed two runs in five innings while striking out nine Twins. He helped the Jays to a 7-3 win.

The Jays finished Week 22 with a 5-1 mark, 79-58 overall. That same week, Joe Carter recorded his 100th RBI and 30th home run. Jack Morris won his eighteenth game, going 14-2 in his last 18 starts. The Jays were steamrolling toward another division title.

Toronto did not let up the following week. David Cone tossed a 1-0 shutout against the Royals in Kansas City. He gave up five hits and struck out five in over eight innings. Jack Morris set a club record with his nineteenth victory. The Jays finished Week 23 with a 5-2 mark, 84-60 overall. They clinched their tenth consecutive winning season, the longest current streak in baseball.

Dave Winfield hit a personal milestone in Week 24 at Toronto. After hitting a three-run homer in a 13-0 victory over Texas on September 18, Winfield had 1,700 career RBIs.

Morris failed his first try to become a 20-game winner for the third time. Still, the Jays won 7-5 in 10 innings against the Cleveland

Indians. With an 88-63 record, Toronto was on the verge of clinching their second division title.

The surprising Milwaukee Brewers were pressing the Jays into Week 25. But the Jays refused to buckle under the pressure. They had been in this position before, and were confident they would not falter like they had in 1987. That year, Detroit swept the Jays in the final series of the season. Toronto lost the title to the Tigers.

"This is the most relaxed and confident team I've ever seen in September," said Rance Mulliniks.

| Standings | | | | |
|---|---|---|---|---|
| Through games of September 20 | | | | |
| EASTERN DIVISION | | | | |
| Club | W | L | Pct. | GB |
| Toronto | 88 | 63 | .583 | — |
| Milwaukee | 83 | 66 | .557 | 4 |
| Baltimore | 81 | 67 | .547 | 5.5 |
| Cleveland | 70 | 79 | .470 | 17 |
| Detroit | 70 | 79 | .470 | 17 |
| New York | 70 | 79 | .470 | 17 |
| Boston | 67 | 92 | .450 | 20 |

"There isn't any comparison to 1987," added Tom Henke.

The Jays finished the week with a 4-2 mark. David Cone tossed a 3-1 victory in New York against the Yankees. Dave Winfield drove in four runs against he Orioles in another win. Winfield became the first player in his 40s to reach the 100-RBI mark.

"The guy's 40 years old," said Joe Carter, "but he plays like he's 28 or 29."

The Toronto Blue Jays clinched the American League East title in the final week of the season. Juan Guzman held Detroit to one hit and no runs over eight innings for the clinching win. It was their third title in four years. Toronto finished Week 26 with a 4-1 mark, 96-66 overall, and a 4-game lead over the Milwaukee Brewers.

Jack Morris finished with a 21-6 record, tying Kevin Brown of the Texas Rangers for the most pitching victories in 1992. Morris also set a club record for victories. Juan Guzman finished with a 16-5 record

*Derek Bell helped Toronto clinch their division*
*in the last week of the season.*

with a 2.64 ERA. And Tom Henke pitched in with 34 saves.

Joe Carter had another great year. He led the team with 34 home runs and 119 RBIs. Dave Winfield had one of his best seasons. He was second on the team in hitting with a .290 average. He also hit 26 home runs and drove in 108 runs. And Roberto Alomar hit a team-best .310 with 76 RBIs.

| Final Standings | | | | |
|---|---|---|---|---|
| Through games of October 4 | | | | |
| EASTERN DIVISION | | | | |
| Club | W | L | Pct. | GB |
| **Toronto** | **96** | **66** | **.593** | **—** |
| Milwaukee | 92 | 70 | .568 | 4 |
| Baltimore | 89 | 73 | .549 | 7 |
| Cleveland | 76 | 86 | .469 | 20 |
| New York | 76 | 86 | .469 | 20 |
| Detroit | 75 | 87 | .463 | 21 |
| Boston | 73 | 89 | .451 | 23 |

The Jays were pleased with their season, but there was no great celebration. They still had much work to do if they wanted to be the first Canadian team to reach the World Series.

*Kelly Gruger's two-run homer in the fifth inning of Game 2
gave Toronto all the offense it would need.*

# Chasing the Pennant

The Blue Jays were heavy favorites to beat the Oakland A's in the playoffs. After all, Toronto had dominant pitchers Morris, Cone, and Guzman. The A's could not match them on paper. But the Jays' better statistics did not guarantee them victory.

In 1985, the Jays had a strong team. They won their division and faced a weaker Kansas City team in the playoffs. The Blue Jays took a 3-1 lead in games—then lost in seven games. The playoff loss saddled the team with the "choker" label. The Jays were eager to finally remove the label by capturing the pennant and winning the World Series.

Jack Morris started Game 1 in Toronto. He had a good record in the playoffs, and Toronto fans anticipated a victory. But Morris struggled the entire game. When Oakland DH Harold Baines hit a game-winning ninth inning home run off Morris,

| Championship Series—Game 1 | | | |
|---|---|---|---|
| Oakland | 030 | 000 | 001—4 |
| Toronto | 000 | 011 | 010—3 |

| Championship Series—Game 2 | | | |
|---|---|---|---|
| Oakland | 000 | 000 | 001—1 |
| Toronto | 000 | 020 | 10x—3 |

the Toronto fans fell silent. It was happening again. Choke!

But this was not 1985. And the Toronto Blue Jays were not the same team. David Cone started Game 2 and held the A's in check. Toronto won the game 3-1. The series was tied 1-1.

Now the series shifted to Oakland. Oakland fans were hoping that the Jays would falter away from the Skydome. But the Jays were determined not the let the series get away.

Toronto led 3-2 going into the top of the seventh. The A's turned the game over to their bullpen—the strength of their team. But the Blue Jays scored two more runs and led 5-2. Oakland responded with two runs of their own in the bottom of the seventh, cutting the lead to 5-4.  The Jays and A's scored a run each in the eighth, making it 6-5.  The Jays finished the scoring with another run in the ninth for a 7-5 victory and a 2-1 series lead.

What made the victory remarkable was the way Toronto hit the A's bullpen.  Jeff Russell was hit hard.  Rick Honeycutt was hit hard.  And most importantly, Dennis Eckersley—the Eck— was hit hard.

| Championship Series—Game 3 | | | |
|---|---|---|---|
| Toronto | 010 | 110 | 211—7 |
| Oakland | 000 | 200 | 210—5 |

During the regular season, Eckersley had 51 saves in 54 opportunities.  He would go on to win the Cy Young Award for best pitcher of the year and would also be named the American League's Most Valuable Player.  Toronto didn't care about the Eck.  They wanted to go to the World Series.

The next night, the A's took a commanding 6-1 lead going into the eighth inning.  But Oakland pitcher Bob Welsh was running out of steam.  Roberto Alomar led off the inning with a double.  Joe Carter and Dave Winfield followed with singles, making it 6-2.  Not wishing to take any more chances with the other pitchers in his bullpen, Oakland Manager Tony LaRussa sent in Eckersley.  It was the earliest Eckersley had entered a game all season.

Eckersley faced John Olerud.  Olerud greeted him with a single, making the score 6-3. Candy Maldonado hit the next pitch to right-center.  Now the score was 6-4. Miraculously, Eckersley retired the next three Toronto batters.  But there was one more inning to play.

Oakland failed to score in the bottom of the eighth.  Devon White led off the ninth inning with a single.  Roberto Alomar hit a screaming line drive down the left field line, but it landed two feet foul.  Eckersley decided to try to blow a fastball past Alomar.  But Alomar

*Manuel Lee avoids a sliding Lance Blankenship in Game 3.*

stung the ball into the right-field seats. The Oakland fans were in shock. Toronto had tied the score off the Eck.

The game went into extra innings. Finally, Toronto scored the game winner in the top of the eleventh inning. They led the series 3-1.

| Championship Series—Game 4 | | | |
|---|---|---|---|
| Toronto | 010 | 000 | 032 | 01—7 |
| Oakland | 005 | 001 | 000 | 00—6 |

"Choke no more," said Joe Carter. "All we've heard about all season is that we choke. Not this time."

But the Blue Jays had been up 3-1 before and lost. They still needed one more victory to reach the World Series.

Toronto lost Game 5 in Oakland. But they led the series 3-2 with the final two games to be played in Toronto.

| Championship Series—Game 5 | | | |
|---|---|---|---|
| Toronto | 000 | 100 | 100—2 |
| Oakland | 201 | 030 | 00x—6 |

In Game 6, Carter started the scoring in the bottom of the first inning when he stroked a two-run homer. In

| Championship Series—Game 6 | | | |
|---|---|---|---|
| Oakland | 000 | 001 | 010—2 |
| Toronto | 204 | 010 | 02x—9 |

the third inning, Candy Maldonado hit a three-run homer. Toronto took a quick 6-0 lead and never looked back. There was no suspense, no drama. The game had already been decided in the first few innings. Toronto went on to win 9-2 and capture their first American League pennant. It was the first time a team outside the United States had made it to the World Series. The city of Toronto erupted in celebration.

*Roberto Alomar was named MVP of the Championship series.*

"We've been so close for so long and had lived with so many negative tags," said Cito Gaston. "We probably don't appreciate what they've done. But it was an exhausting series, emotional, exhausting and fiery. It was as intense as baseball gets as every game seemed to go back and forth across the line of dislike and respect."

Roberto Alomar was named MVP of the American League Championship Series. He hit .423 with two home runs and four RBIs. Now came the ultimate test. Could the Blue Jays win their first-ever World Series?

# The World Series

The Blue Jays' opponent was the Atlanta Braves. Atlanta had made it to the World Series in 1991, only to lose to Jack Morris and the Minnesota Twins in a classic seven-game showdown. Atlanta had World Series experience. And they too were eager to avenge their previous postseason losses.

The Series opened in Atlanta. Morris and Tom Glavine locked in a pitching duel. Joe Carter started the

| The World Series—Game 1 | | | |
|---|---|---|---|
| Toronto | 000 | 100 | 000—1 |
| Atlanta | 000 | 003 | 00x—3 |

scoring with a solo home run in the fourth. But Atlanta catcher Damon Berryhill responded by hitting a hanging forkball for a three-run homer in the sixth inning. That was all the scoring, and Atlanta took Game 1.

*Joe Carter hits a home run in Game 1 of the World Series.*

During the singing of the Canadian anthem before Game 2, a U.S. Marine accidentally presented the Canadian flag upside down. Irate Canadian citizens flooded the telephone lines to Atlanta's Fulton County Stadium, protesting the display. The Atlanta Braves later apologized for the error. But some Canadians felt it was a deliberate display from a country afraid of losing its national game to another country.

In Game 2, the Braves chipped away at David Cone. They took a 2-0 lead into the fifth inning before the Jays tied the game. Atlanta responded by scoring 2 runs in the bottom of the inning. Heading into the top of the ninth inning, the Braves led 4-3. It looked like they were about to take a 2-0 series lead.

Atlanta Manager Bobby Cox brought in relief ace Jeff Reardon. Reardon got the first out, but then walked Derek Bell. Cito Gaston sent Ed Sprague to pinch hit. The young catcher smashed a Reardon fastball deep into the left field stands for a 5-4 Toronto lead. Tom Henke closed the door on Atlanta in the bottom of the inning, and the series shifted to Toronto tied at 1-1.

| The World Series—Game 2 | | | |
|---|---|---|---|
| Toronto | 000 | 020 | 012—5 |
| Atlanta | 010 | 120 | 000—4 |

Game 3 was another pitching duel. With no one out in the fourth inning of a scoreless game, Atlanta had runners on base. Deion Sanders was on second and Terry Pendleton was on first. David Justice slashed a line drive to the center field fence.

Devon White streaked back, leaped high and caught the ball. Then he threw a perfect strike to the relay man, Roberto Alomar. Terry Pendleton was off and running at the crack of the bat. Deion Sanders stood on second base to tag up. Pendleton passed Sanders and was called out. Then Sanders took off for third and was caught in a run-down. Kelly Gruber tagged Sanders as he slid back into second. But Sanders was called safe.

Gruber tied the game 2-2 with an eighth-inning home run. It ended his postseason-record 0-for-23 slump. In the bottom of the ninth, Candy Maldonado singled with two outs and the bases loaded for a 3-2 Blue Jay win. Toronto had grabbed a 2-1 series lead.

In Game 4, Toronto sent Jimmy Key to the mound. He pitched seven strong innings before turning the ball over to Duane Ward. Henke mopped up in the top of the ninth inning to preserve a 2-1 Toronto win. Now the Blue Jays were one victory away from the championship.

| The World Series—Game 3 | | | |
|---|---|---|---|
| Atlanta | 000 | 001 | 010—2 |
| Toronto | 000 | 100 | 011—3 |

| The World Series—Game 4 | | | |
|---|---|---|---|
| Atlanta | 000 | 000 | 010—1 |
| Toronto | 001 | 000 | 10x—2 |

*Candy Maldonado strokes the winning hit in Game 3.*

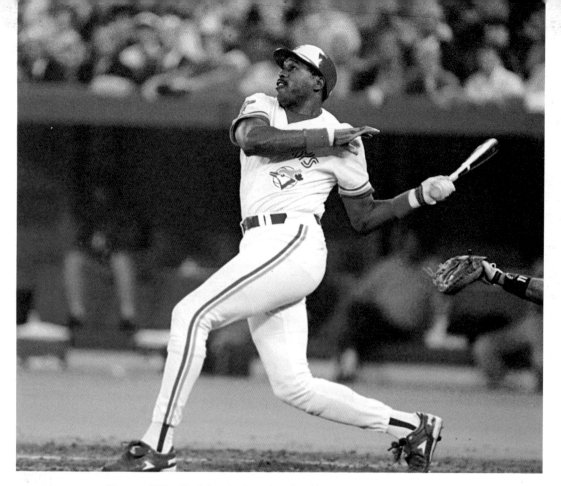

*Dave Winfield stings the ball in a Game-5 loss.*

The city of Toronto made plans for a victory parade after Game 5 in Toronto. After all, Jack Morris was pitching. But Terry Pendleton dashed those plans with a fifth-inning grand slam, breaking open a close game. The Braves went on to an easy 7-2 win. Games 6 and 7 would be played in Atlanta.

| The World Series—Game 5 | | | |
|---|---|---|---|
| Atlanta | 100 | 150 | 000—7 |
| Toronto | 010 | 100 | 000—2 |

Toronto fans feared a repeat of 1985. But the Blue Jays had other ideas. In Game 6, Candy Maldonado gave the Jays a 2-1 lead in the fourth inning. David Cone and a string of relievers held the Braves in check until the ninth inning. Then Gaston sent in Tom Henke to close out the game. But Atlanta's Otis Nixon hit a two-out single off Henke to tie the game and send it into extra innings.

32

*Tom Henke could not hold off Atlanta in the 9th inning of Game 6.*

Jimmy Key came on to pitch the bottom of the tenth inning and held the Braves scoreless. In the top of the eleventh with two out, Devon White was on second and Roberto Alomar was on first. Dave Winfield stood at the plate facing Charlie Liebrandt. Winfield worked his way to a 3-2 count. Then he smashed a Liebrandt change-up into the left-field corner for a double. Two runs scored for a 4-2 Blue Jay lead.

But in the bottom of the eleventh, Atlanta rallied to put runners on first and third with no outs. Toronto fans held their breath once more. Would the Jays choke under pressure?

Atlanta sacrificed a runner to second. Now there were Braves on second and third with one out. A base hit would probably tie the game.

A ground ball out scored Atlanta's third run and moved a runner to third. But now there were two outs. Speedy Otis Nixon stepped to the plate. Cito Gaston removed Key and brought in fireballer Mike Timlin. Timlin had been hurt much of the year and wasn't much of a factor. But for the playoffs, he was healthy. And his fastball was never better.

Timlin blew one fastball by Nixon on the inside corner. Then Timlin wound up and fired again. Nixon reached his bat out to bunt. He pulled the ball towards first base. But Timlin rushed off the mound and intercepted the ball. He threw it to Joe Carter at first base for the

| The World Series—Game 6 | | | | |
| --- | --- | --- | --- | --- |
| Toronto | 100 | 100 | 000 | 02—4 |
| Atlanta | 001 | 000 | 001 | 01—3 |

final out. Carter jumped twice, looked back to make sure Nixon was out, then kept jumping. The Toronto Blue Jays were World Series Champions. The celebration had begun.

Pat Borders was named World Series MVP. He hit .450 with one home run and three runs batted in.

*Jimmy Key held the Braves scoreless in the 10th inning of game 6.*

"This is the best team I've ever played on," said Dave Winfield. "It just took a true team to finally win. We overcame a lot, overcame all the labels, overcame all the odds. It's the culmination of a great year."

"I'm happy for our fans," said Joe Carter. "I'm happy for ourselves. This will put to rest a lot of talk about the Toronto Blue Jays."

"No one can say we choke anymore," added Roberto Alomar. "This is a great club. We won like champions."

*Pat Borders was named World Series MVP.*

# Final Major League Standings
## 1992
### Eastern Division

|  | W | L | Pct. | GB | Home | Away |
|---|---|---|---|---|---|---|
| **Toronto** | **96** | **66** | **.593** | — | **53-28** | **43-38** |
| Milwaukee | 92 | 70 | .568 | 4 | 53-28 | 39-42 |
| Baltimore | 89 | 73 | .549 | 7 | 43-38 | 46-35 |
| Cleveland | 76 | 86 | .469 | 20 | 41-40 | 35-46 |
| New York | 76 | 86 | .469 | 20 | 41-40 | 35-46 |
| Detroit | 75 | 86 | .463 | 21 | 38-42 | 37-45 |
| Boston | 73 | 89 | .451 | 23 | 44-37 | 29-52 |

*W—Wins* • *L—Losses* • *Pct.—Percentage* • *GB—Games Behind*

## Toronto Blue Jays

| Batting | Avg. | AB | R | H | HR | RBI | SB |
|---|---|---|---|---|---|---|---|
| Roberto Alomar | **.310** | 571 | **105** | **177** | 8 | 76 | **49** |
| Dave Winfield | .290 | 583 | 92 | 169 | 26 | 108 | 2 |
| John Olerud | .284 | 458 | 68 | 130 | 16 | 66 | 1 |
| Candy Maldonado | .272 | 489 | 64 | 133 | 20 | 66 | 2 |
| Joe Carter | .264 | 622 | 97 | 164 | **34** | **119** | 12 |
| Manuel Lee | .263 | 396 | 49 | 104 | 3 | 39 | 6 |
| Randy Knorr | .263 | 19 | 1 | 5 | 1 | 2 | 0 |
| Devon White | .248 | **641** | 98 | 159 | 17 | 60 | 37 |
| Derek Bell | .242 | 161 | 23 | 39 | 2 | 15 | 7 |
| Pat Borders | .242 | 480 | 47 | 116 | 13 | 53 | 1 |
| Jeff Kent | .240 | 192 | 36 | 46 | 8 | 35 | 2 |
| Ed Sprague | .234 | 47 | 6 | 11 | 1 | 7 | 0 |
| Alfredo Griffin | .233 | 150 | 21 | 35 | 0 | 10 | 3 |
| Kelly Gruber | .229 | 446 | 42 | 102 | 11 | 43 | 7 |

***Bold—Team Leader*** • *Avg.—Average* • *AB—At Bat* • *R—Runs* • *H—Hits*
*HR—Home Runs* • *RBI—Runs Batted In* • *SB—Stolen Bases*

| Pitcher | ERA | W-L | Gm | IP | BB | SO |
|---|---|---|---|---|---|---|
| Duane Ward | **1.95** | 7-4 | **79** | 101.1 | 39 | 103 |
| Tom Henke | 2.26 | 3-2 | 57 | 55.2 | 22 | 46 |
| David Cone | 2.55 | 4-3 | 8 | 53.0 | 29 | 47 |
| Juan Guzman | 2.64 | 16-5 | 28 | 180.2 | 72 | **165** |
| Mark Eichorn | 3.08 | 4-4 | 65 | 87.2 | 25 | 61 |
| Jimmy Key | 3.53 | 13-13 | 33 | 216.2 | 59 | 117 |
| Jack Morris | 4.04 | **21-6** | 34 | **240.2** | **80** | 132 |
| Mike Timlin | 4.12 | 0-2 | 26 | 43.2 | 20 | 35 |
| Bob MacDonald | 4.37 | 1-0 | 27 | 47.1 | 16 | 26 |
| Todd Stottlemyre | 4.50 | 12-11 | 28 | 174.0 | 63 | 98 |
| Dave Stieb | 5.04 | 4-6 | 21 | 96.1 | 43 | 45 |
| Pat Hentgen | 5.36 | 5-2 | 28 | 50.1 | 32 | 39 |
| David Wells | 5.40 | 7-9 | 41 | 120.0 | 36 | 62 |

*Bold—Team Leader* • *W-L—Wins/Losses* • *Gm—Games*
*IP—Innings Pitched* • *BB—Base on Balls* • *SO—Strike Outs*

*Roberto Alomar led the team in hitting.*

*Duane Ward had the team's best earned run average (E.R.A.)*

# GLOSSARY

**Balk**— an illegal act by the pitcher with a runner or runners on base, entitling all runners to advance one base.

**Ball**—a pitch which does not enter the strike zone in flight and is not struck at by the batter.

**Base**—one of four points which must be touched by a runner in order to score a run.

**Base On Balls**—an award of first base granted to a batter who, during his or her time at bat, receives four pitches outside the strike zone.

**Batter**—an offensive player who takes his or her position in the batter's box.

**Batter's Box**—the area within which the batter stands during his or her time at bat.

**Battery**—the pitcher and the catcher.

**Bunt**—a batted ball not swung at, but intentionally met with the bat and tapped slowly within the infield.

**Catcher**—the fielder who takes his or her position back of the home base.

**Dead Ball**—a ball out of play because of a legally created temporary suspension of play.

**Double-Header**—two regularly scheduled or rescheduled games played in immediate succession.

**Double Play**—a play by the defense in which two offensive players are put out as a result of continuous action, providing there is no error between putouts.

**Fair Territory**—part of the playing field within, and including the first base and third base lines, from home base to the bottom of the playing field fence and upwards. All foul lines are in fair territory.

**Fielder**—any defensive player.

**Fielder's Choice**—the act of a fielder who handles a fair grounder and, instead of throwing to first base to put out the batter-runner, throws to another base in an attempt to put out a preceding runner.

**Fly Ball**—a batted ball that goes high in the air in flight.

**Force Play**—a play in which a runner legally loses his or her right to occupy a base by reason of the batter becoming a runner.

**Foul Territory**—part of the playing field outside the first and third base lines extended to the fence and upwards.

**Foul Tip**—a batted ball that goes sharp and direct from the bat to the catcher's hands and is legally caught.

**Ground Ball**— a batted ball that rolls or bounces close to the ground.

**Infielder**—a fielder who occupies a position in the infield.

**Inning**—a portion of the game within which the teams alternate on offense and defense and in which there are three putouts for each team. Each team's time at bat is a half-inning.

**Line Drive**—a batted ball that goes sharp and direct from the bat to a fielder without touching the ground.

**Offense**—the team, or any player of the team, at bat.

**Out**—one of the three required retirements of an offensive team during its time at bat.

**Outfielder**—a fielder who occupies a position in the outfield, which is the area of the playing field most distant from home base.

**Pitch**—a ball delivered to the batter by the pitcher.

**Pitcher**—the fielder designated to deliver the pitch to the batter.

**Run**—the score made by an offensive player who advances from batter to runner and touches first, second, third, and home bases in that order.

**Run-down**—the act of the defense in an attempt to put out a runner between bases.

**Runner**—an offensive player who is advancing toward, or touching, or returning to any base.

**"Safe"**—a declaration by the umpire that a runner is entitled to the base for which he or she was trying.

**Set Position**—one of the two legal pitching positions.

**Squeeze Play**—a play when a team, with a runner on third base, attempts to score that runner by means of a bunt.

**Strike**—a legal pitch when so called by the umpire that is struck at by the batter and is missed; is not struck at, if any part of the ball passes through any part of the strike zone; is fouled by the batter when he or she has less than two strikes; is bunted foul; touches the batter as he or she strikes at it; touches the batter in flight in the strike zone; or becomes a foul tip.

**Strike Zone**—the area over home plate the upper limit of which is a horizontal line at the midpoint between the top of the shoulders and the top of the uniform pants, and the lower level is a line at the top of the knees.

**Triple Play**—a play by the defense in which three offensive players are put out as a result of continuous action, providing there is no error between putouts.

**Wild Pitch**—a pitch so high, so low, or so wide of the plate that it cannot be handled with ordinary effort by the catcher.

**Wind-Up Position**—one of the two legal pitching positions.